EXPLORE
SOLIDS
AND
LIQUIDS!

Kathleen M. Reilly

Illustrated by Bryan Stone

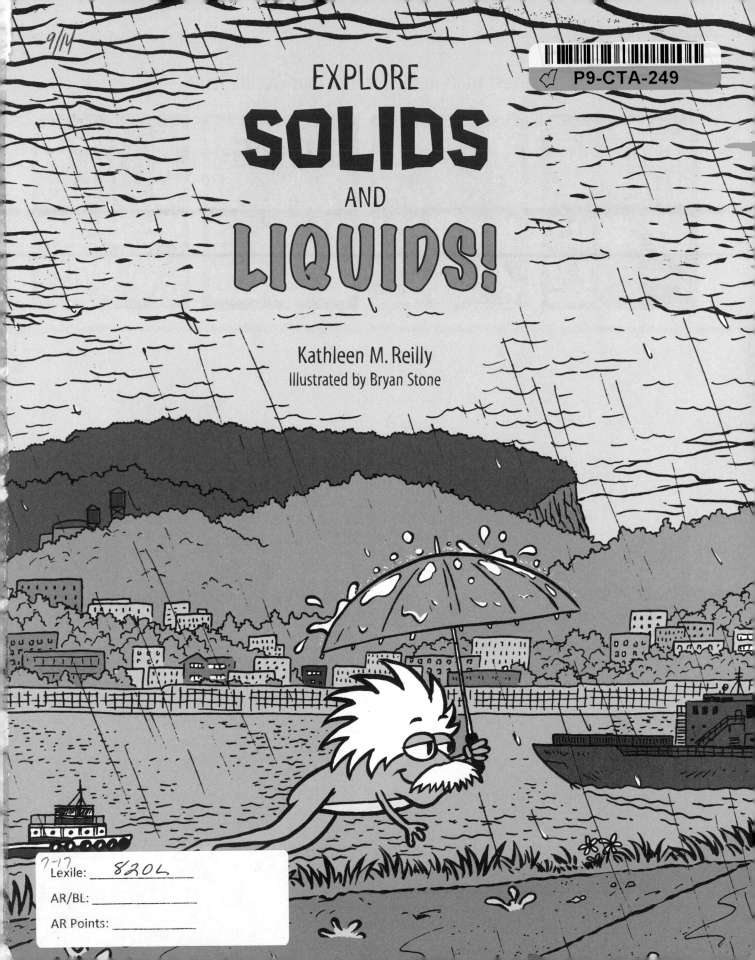

Newest titles in the **Explore Your World!** Series

Nomad Press
A division of Nomad Communications
10 9 8 7 6 5 4 3 2 1
Copyright © 2014 by Nomad Press. All rights reserved.

This book was manufactured by TC Transcontinental Printing,
Beauceville Québec, Canada
August 2014, Job #67278
ISBN: 978-1-61930-237-2

Illustrations by Bryan Stone
Educational Consultant, Marla Conn

Questions regarding the ordering of this book should be addressed to
Nomad Press
2456 Christian St.
White River Junction, VT 05001
www.nomadpress.net

Printed in Canada.

CONTENTS

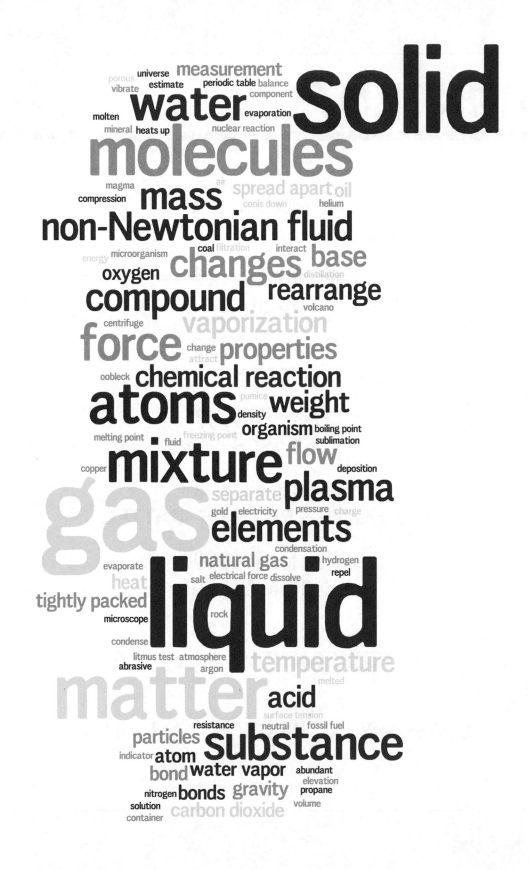

MATTER REALLY MATTERS

How is a cat like a car? Or a marshmallow like your swing set? These aren't riddles—it's science! The answer to these funny questions is that all these things are made of **matter**. In fact, everything in the **universe** is made of matter.

SO WHAT IS MATTER?

Matter is everything around you. The chair you're sitting in, this book, your clothes, the water you washed your hands in—even the air you're breathing right now! The ice cube in your drink, the lemonade in your glass, and the steam coming out of the tea kettle—these solids, liquids, and gases are all matter.

Anything that takes up space is considered matter.

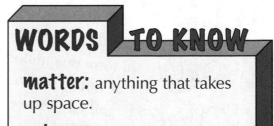

WORDS TO KNOW

matter: anything that takes up space.

universe: everything that exists, everywhere.

What is matter made of? If you could zoom in for a really close look, you'd see that matter is made up of very small **particles** called **atoms**.

Particles are tiny pieces of matter, and atoms are very small particles. They're so small, you need a super powerful microscope just to see them. Atoms are the building blocks of all matter.

When atoms join together, they form a cluster of atoms called a **molecule**. All matter is made up of molecules. Imagine an atom is a letter of the alphabet, such as the letter S. If you combine it with other letters (or atoms)—such as U and N—you get the word (or molecule) SUN.

WORDS TO KNOW

particle: a tiny piece of matter.

atom: a very small piece of matter. Atoms make up everything in the universe.

molecule: a group of atoms.

hydrogen: an element that is a gas in the air. It is the most common element.

oxygen: an element that is a gas in the air. People and animals need oxygen to breathe.

element: a pure **substance** that is made of atoms that are all the same.

substance: a kind of matter.

DID YOU KNOW?

Sometimes people call water H_2O (aich-two-oh). That's because two **hydrogen** atoms (the H) combine with one **oxygen** atom (the O) to form one molecule of water. Hydrogen and oxygen are **elements**.

$$S + U + N = SUN$$

That's how a molecule works—a group of atoms joins together to make something new. They don't have to be different atoms, either. If you add another S to your word (or molecule), you get SUNS—a different word.

2

MATTER REALLY MATTERS

EXPLORING MATTER

In this book, you'll explore what matter is. You'll learn the different forms matter takes, how it changes, and how you can mix different kinds of matter together.

Understanding matter is the first step to understanding pretty much everything in the physical world! Once you know about matter, you can keep learning more and more about the amazing world you live in.

THAT'S SO DENSE!

Let's start by learning some interesting facts about matter. Matter has something called **mass**. Mass is the measurement of how much space something takes up combined with how tightly its atoms are packed together.

Think of a golf ball and a table tennis ball. They're both about the same size. They both take up about the same space. But the table tennis ball has less **density**.

This means the atoms inside the table tennis ball are farther apart. It's filled with air, and those air molecules are spread apart inside it. The golf ball has much greater density. That's because the molecules that make it up are packed together very tightly.

mass: the measurement of how many atoms are in matter and how tightly packed the atoms are.

density: how tightly packed or spread apart molecules are in matter.

3

"WEIGHT" A MINUTE

The golf ball is heavier than the table tennis ball. But mass is NOT the same as **weight**. Weight is the measurement of how much an object is being pulled down by the **force** of **gravity**. How do you weigh yourself? You step on a scale and see how much **pressure** is made on the scale when gravity pulls you down.

Here on Earth, mass and weight are pretty similar. But what if you took those two balls to outer space, where there is no gravity? Without any gravity, what would change?

The masses of those balls would stay the same. Each ball still has the same number of atoms inside, still packed together with the same density each had on Earth. But the weights would change, they would become lighter because there would be no gravity pulling them down.

WORDS TO KNOW

weight: the measurement of gravity pulling down on matter.

force: a push or a pull.

gravity: a force that pulls all objects to the earth.

pressure: a force that pushes on an object.

BACK TO BASICS

How many letters are in the alphabet? Just 26 letters in the English alphabet combine to make all of our words. It works the same way with atoms and molecules. The different types of atoms combine to make up all kinds of molecules, which make up all kinds of matter.

What is an element? An element is a pure substance that's made of just one type of atom. Gold is made of gold atoms. Oxygen is made of oxygen atoms. But water is made of oxygen atoms combined with hydrogen atoms, which form water molecules.

WORDS TO KNOW

periodic table: the chart that shows all the known elements.

To organize all the elements, scientists created a chart called the **periodic table**. This chart shows every known element. As you can see, H is for hydrogen and O is for oxygen. Can you find the symbol for gold? Hint: it isn't the letter "G." Can you find any other elements you've heard of?

PERIODIC TABLE OF ELEMENTS

H Hydrogen	He Helium

Li Lithium	Be Beryllium		B Boron	C Carbon	N Nitrogen	O Oxygen	F Fluorine	Ne Neon

Na Sodium, Mg Magnesium, Al Aluminum, Si Silicon, P Phosphorus, S Sulfur, Cl Chlorine, Ar Argon

K Potassium, Ca Calcium, Sc Scandium, Ti Titanium, V Vanadium, Cr Chromium, Mn Manganese, Fe Iron, Co Cobalt, Ni Nickel, Cu Copper, Zn Zinc, Ga Gallium, Ge Germanium, As Arsenic, Se Selenium, Br Bromine, Kr Krypton

Rb Rubidium, Sr Strontium, Y Yttrium, Zr Zirconium, Nb Niobium, Mo Molybdenum, Tc Technetium, Ru Ruthenium, Rh Rhodium, Pd Palladium, Ag Silver, Cd Cadmium, In Indium, Sn Tin, Sb Antimony, Te Tellurium, I Iodine, Xe Xenon

Cs Cesium, Ba Barium, La Lanthanum, Hf Hafnium, Ta Tantalum, W Tungsten, Re Rhenium, Os Osmium, Ir Iridium, Pt Platinum, Au Gold, Hg Mercury, Tl Thallium, Pb Lead, Bi Bismuth, Po Polonium, At Astatine, Rn Radon

Fr Francium, Ra Radium, Ac Actinium, Rf Rutherfordium, Ha Hahnium, Sg Seaborgium, Bh Bohrium, Hs Hassium, Mt Meitnerium

Ce Cerium, Pr Praseodymium, Nd Neodymium, Pm Promethium, Sm Samarium, Eu Europium, Gd Gadolinium, Tb Terbium, Dy Dysprosium, Ho Holmium, Er Erbium, Tm Thulium, Yb Ytterbium, Lu Lutetium

Th Thorium, Pa Protactinium, U Uranium, Np Neptunium, Pu Plutonium, Am Americium, Cm Curium, Bk Berkelium, Cf Californium, Es Einsteinium, Fm Fermium, Md Mendelevium, No Nobelium, Lr Lawrencium

Scientists are still discovering new elements. While this book was being written, scientists proposed a new element for the 115th position. It still has its temporary name, ununpentium, which means *one, one, five* in Latin.

DANCING MOLECULES

Atoms and molecules move! How is that possible? You can't see them moving just by looking at an object, because atoms and molecules are way too tiny to be seen with your eyes.

Hold a rock in your hand and take a good look at it. It's definitely not moving, right? But if you take a tiny piece of that rock and put it under a high-powered microscope, you'd actually see the molecules moving around. And if that piece of rock is heated up, the molecules will move even faster.

WORDS TO KNOW

dissolve: when molecules of one substance get mixed into the molecules of another substance.

What happens when you mix a powdered drink with water? The powder seems to disappear and the water takes on that flavor, right? But the powder didn't really disappear. Instead, it **dissolved** into the water. That means the molecules of powder moved around and spread out among the molecules of water.

IT'S THE STATE OF THE MATTER

Is matter all the same? No! Matter can take different forms, including solids, liquids, and gases. You'll explore these states of matter in upcoming chapters, along with other, less common forms of matter. Remember those molecules that make up matter?

Why can't you trust atoms?

LAUGH IT UP!

They make up everything!

Density, or how closely the molecules are packed together, is what decides the form of that matter.

SOLID: The particles of a solid are packed very tightly together. If you take an empty jar and put a wooden block in it, that block will just sit there because it's solid. The block is not going to change at all. That's because the molecules are clustered very tightly together inside the block. The only way you can change that block is to chop it up or burn it!

LIQUID: The molecules inside a liquid aren't as tightly packed together as they are in a solid. Water, juice, and milk are all liquids. If you take that same empty jar and put water inside it, what will happen? The water will move around until it takes on the shape of that jar. The same thing will happen if you pour that water into a plastic bag—the water will take on the shape of the bag.

GAS: The molecules in a gas are even more spread out. Think about that empty jar again. Is it really empty? It's actually filled with air! Air is a gas. Gases have no real shape, but a gas takes up the entire space of the container it's in. When water takes the shape of the jar, it doesn't spread out to totally fill it. You can fill a jar halfway up, right? But a gas spreads throughout the whole container.

Picture it like this: If you're hugging someone tightly, you're like two molecules packed close together. You're like a solid! But if you walk along holding hands, you're a little more loosely connected, like liquid molecules. And if you're dancing near each other but not touching, you're like two gas molecules!

SOLID   LIQUID   GAS

TIGHTLY PACKED   LOOSELY CONNECTED   NEAR EACH OTHER

Of all the known elements, hydrogen is the most abundant. It makes up about 75 percent of the universe.

Can an object change from one form of matter to another? Think about water. It can get really cold and change from a liquid to solid ice. It can also get really hot and change from a liquid to steam, which is a gas. We're going to have fun learning about matter!

NO ROOM FOR YOU!

> science notebook
> pen or pencil
> clear jar with lid
> small ball, marble, or rock
> dry rice or unpopped popcorn

If you're sitting in a chair and a friend tries to join you, what happens? Can two objects be in the same space at once? Do this project to find out!

1 Before beginning, start a scientific method worksheet like the one shown here. The scientific method is the way scientists ask questions and find answers. Choose a notebook to use as your science notebook for the activities in this book.

2 Place the small ball or other small object into the jar. Fill the jar with the rice or popcorn up to about 2 inches (5 centimeters) from the top. This will completely cover the ball. Replace the lid.

3 Gently shake the jar back and forth, not up and down. What do you see happening to the rice and the ball as you keep shaking? Why do you think that they move in this way?

SCIENTIFIC METHOD WORKSHEET

QUESTION: What are we trying to find out? What problem are we trying to solve?

RESEARCH: What do other people think about this question?

HYPOTHESIS/PREDICTION: What do we think the answer will be?

EQUIPMENT: What supplies are we using?

METHOD: What steps are we following?

RESULTS: What happened and why?

WHAT'S HAPPENING? As you shake the jar, the rice shifts around until there's very little air space left between each grain. While the rice moves around and gets closer together, it pushes the ball upward. Why does this happen?

PROJECT

9

SUPPLIES

- small pot
- 1 cup (236 milliliters) water
- 1½ cups (354 milliliters) sugar to start, then about another ½ cup (118 milliliters) sugar for third step
- wooden spoon
- mason jar or other glass container that can hold hot water
- pencil
- clean cotton string
- scissors

Can molecules move apart and come back together? See if this is possible and then eat the results!
CAUTION: An adult needs to help with the boiling water.

1 Fill the pot with water. Have an adult heat it and remove it from the stove once it's boiling.

2 With your adult helper, add the sugar to the water and stir it until it's completely dissolved. Be careful—it's still going to be very hot! When all the sugar is completely dissolved you shouldn't see any more sugar crystals anywhere.

3 Start adding more sugar, just a little at a time. Keep stirring! You should notice that it takes longer for the sugar to dissolve each time you add more. Stop adding sugar once you can see sugar floating in the water. This should take about another ½ cup of sugar, but keep watching and adjust to what you observe. Let the sugar water cool for about 10 minutes.

4 While the sugar water is cooling, tie one end of the string around your pencil. Lay the pencil across the top of your jar. Cut the string to a length that will just let it reach the bottom of your jar. Once you've got a good length, take the pencil and string off the jar and set it aside.

5 When your water has cooled, pour it into your jar.

10

6 Take a little sugar and rub it onto the dry string. This will give your rock candy crystals something to grab onto.

7 Lay the pencil back over the glass so the string hangs down into the water. Poke the string down a little if it tries to float. You want it hanging down into the glass.

8 Now comes the hard part. Put your jar in a place where it won't get bumped, and wait! What do you notice after two days? Check every day for a week. It's worth the wait!

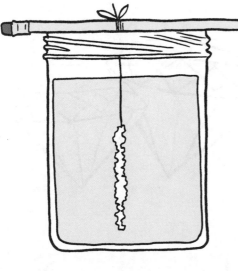

THINGS TO THINK ABOUT: What do you think happened to the sugar molecules when they dissolved in the hot water? What did those same molecules do as the water cooled?

PROJECT

11

UNFILLABLE BALLOON

Can something invisible be made of matter? Air is matter, even though you can't see it. In this project, you can see invisible matter in action by experimenting with an empty bottle. Wait a minute! Is that bottle really empty? Or is it filled with . . . air?

1 Start a scientific method worksheet in your science notebook.

2 Insert the balloon into the neck of the empty soda bottle. Fold the neck of the balloon over the outside of the bottle a little so it stays in place. Try to blow up the balloon.

3 What happens when you try to blow up the balloon? Why do you think this happens? What is already inside the jar that keeps the balloon from blowing up? Record your discoveries in your science notebook.

WHAT'S HAPPENING? Air is made up of matter and has mass. It takes up space inside the bottle. So when you try to fill the balloon with air, there is no room for that new air to go. Even gases can't be in the same space at the same time.

DID YOU KNOW?

Although most matter is made up of different elements, some are made from only one. Pure diamonds have only one element—carbon!

PROJECT

SOLIDS

If you look around your house, can you see that most of the matter you use in your daily life is solid? That's because solids come in an amazing number of shapes, textures, and sizes. They serve all kinds of purposes, such as the bike you ride, the toothbrush you use to clean your teeth, or this book you're reading.

Something is solid if its molecules are all held so tightly together that the object holds its shape. This is a **property** of a solid. A solid doesn't change its shape based on where it is.

WORDS TO KNOW

property: a quality or feature of something. The way something is.

13

If you put a rock in a bag, it's still going to be the same shape when you take it out of that bag. But you've also seen how solids can be very different from each other. Even similar solids, like two balls, can be different sizes or have different densities. A solid's density depends on how many atoms it has and how closely those atoms are packed together.

CAN'T CHANGE ME!

This doesn't mean that solids cannot change. They can. Solids just need some sort of force applied to them. For instance, what happens if you smash your rock into pieces with a hammer? Now you have a bunch of smaller pieces of rock. It is still the same matter. It still has the same molecules. But the rock's original shape has been changed into smaller shapes.

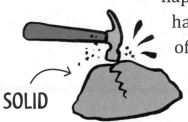

SOLID

STILL A SOLID

WHERE DID IT GO?

If you put a rock in a glass of water, that rock will sit there and be the same rock. Salt and sugar are also solids, but what happens when you stir salt or sugar into that glass of water? These solids seem to disappear. That's because they dissolve. The solid molecules mix with the water molecules and become part of the water. Can any solid dissolve in water? What happens if you mix bits of wood or grains of sand in water? Do they dissolve in the water or settle at the bottom?

Solids can change in other ways, too. As you know, if you heat ice, which is solid water, it will melt and become a liquid. A solid changes into a liquid when it reaches a certain **temperature** called its **melting point**.

WORDS **TO KNOW**

temperature: how warm or cold something is.

melting point: the temperature at which a solid changes into a liquid.

freezing point: the temperature at which a liquid changes into a solid.

SOLID **LIQUID**

Other solids can melt, too. Even rocks can melt if they're super heated! Wax is another solid that you might see melt when it's heated.

Different solids have different melting points. A piece of chocolate is solid at room temperature but starts to melt within a minute of being placed in your hand. Your body heat quickly melts chocolate.

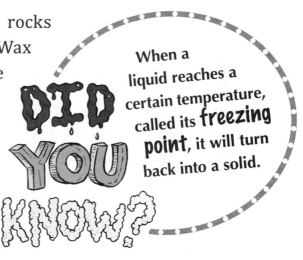

DID YOU KNOW?

When a liquid reaches a certain temperature, called its **freezing point**, it will turn back into a solid.

A stick of butter is also a solid at room temperature, but you need more than the heat of your hand to melt it. To melt butter, you need the heat of the stove or a microwave.

What about an ice cube? At room temperature, water is a liquid. All you need to do to melt an ice cube is take it out of the freezer.

When a solid melts, the molecules of the solid are still there. But they are heated enough to make them start moving around. They move around so much that they take on the properties of liquid. In chapter five, you'll explore different ways that matter—including solids—can change their states.

HOW BIG IS IT?

You can measure solids in a lot of different ways. That's because they stay the same. One way to measure a solid is to find out how long or wide or tall it is. That's when you use a ruler or a measuring tape and measure from one end to the other.

To measure a solid's weight you can weigh it on a bathroom scale. But to measure its mass, you need to use a special scale, called a **balance**. What is the difference between a balance and a bathroom scale?

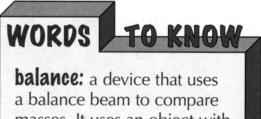

WORDS TO KNOW

balance: a device that uses a balance beam to compare masses. It uses an object with a known mass on one side to measure the mass of the object on the other side.

A bathroom scale has a spring. It measures the force of gravity on an object against the spring. A balance uses a balance beam. It compares masses by balancing your object against the gravity of a known mass. A balance measures in grams or kilograms and will tell you how much matter is in any solid.

On Earth, weight and mass are usually very similar.

MELTING AND FREEZING POINTS

If a liquid gets cold enough, it freezes and turns into a solid. This is its freezing point. Now what happens when this frozen solid starts to get warmer? At some point it melts and turns into a liquid. Can you see why the freezing point and the melting point are the same? It just depends on whether the substance is a liquid turning into a solid (freezing) or a solid turning into a liquid (melting).

Even gases can have a freezing and melting point. If a gas gets colder and colder, at some point it gets so cold that it turns into a liquid. If it keeps getting colder, it gets so cold it freezes. Have you ever had a balloon filled with **helium**? Helium is a gas that makes balloons float. If you've ever been outside with a helium-filled balloon and let go by mistake, you've seen how the helium makes the balloon rise up through the air very quickly. Helium has the lowest melting point of any element: -457 degrees Fahrenheit (-273 degrees Celsius). That's really cold!

Another way to measure a solid is to find out its **volume**. That's how much space the solid takes up. A golf ball has about the same volume as a table tennis ball. That's because they both take up about the same amount of space in your pocket. They have different weight and mass because they are different inside. The table tennis ball has air in it. What is inside a golf ball?

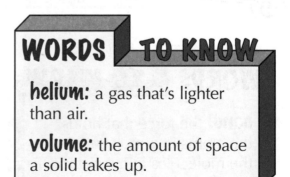

WORDS TO KNOW

helium: a gas that's lighter than air.

volume: the amount of space a solid takes up.

The way you measure volume depends on the shape of the object. If it's a box, you can measure the length, width, and height of the box. Let's say your box is 2 feet long, 1 foot wide, and 1 foot tall (61 by 30 by 30 centimeters). You can use math to figure out the volume. You need to multiply 2 feet times 1 foot times 1 foot = 2 cubic feet (61 x 30 x 30 = 54,900 cubic centimeters). Other shapes are more complicated to measure and calculate.

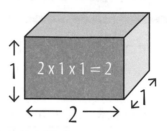

HOW DID THAT HAPPEN?

Using force, solids can be broken into smaller pieces and their shapes can be changed. Think about a rubber band. Imagine stretching it . . . and stretching it . . . keep going . . . until . . . *SNAP!* The rubber band breaks.

Even though the rubber band is stretchy, it's still a solid. When you pull it too far, the **bonds** between its molecules just can't hold together anymore. The bonds break apart.

It's like glass or stiff plastic, too much pressure, and *CRACK!* The bonds are broken and you've got a mess on your hands.

WORDS TO KNOW

bond: the force that holds the atoms in a molecule (or the molecules in a substance) together.

18

> drinking glass
> water
> ice cubes
> string
> salt
> science notebook
> pencil

You know that heat can melt ice. Do you think salt can melt ice, too? Discover it yourself with this activity. Use a scientific method worksheet in your science notebook to organize your experiment.

1 Fill the drinking glass with cold water. Put a couple of ice cubes in the glass with the water.

2 Lay one end of your string across one of the ice cubes. Sprinkle a little bit of salt around the string (not too much!).

3 Wait about 10 or 15 seconds, then lift the string. What happens to the ice cube? How can you explain what happens using what you know about solids and liquids and how they can change from one to the other?

WHAT'S HAPPENING? The salt melted just the very top of the ice cube. It caused the molecules to move around fast enough to turn into water. Then the string settled into that tiny, shallow pool of melted water. But that little pool of water was still sitting on the ice. It got cold enough to make the water molecules slow down again. This froze the water back up and sealed in the string.

You can use this project as a challenge to your friends or family. Tell them, "I can pick up ice with string!" If they doubt you, show them this trick.

DID YOU KNOW?

Carbon is a solid that has the highest melting point at 3,527 degrees Fahrenheit (1,942 degrees Celsius).

PROJECT

> ½ cup (118 milliliters) warm water
> 4 tablespoons (59 milliliters) Epsom salts (from the pharmacy department)
> paintbrush
> black or very dark-colored construction paper

Sometimes it's hard to believe that a solid is still around after it's been dissolved. It seems to have disappeared! This activity will help you see that a solid will still be a solid.

1 Stir the Epsom salts into the water. Keep stirring until it looks like the salts have all dissolved.

2 Dip the paintbrush into the water **mixture** and use it to paint a simple picture (such as a face or a big tree) on the construction paper. Be sure not to soak the paper too much!

3 Set the paper someplace warm and dry. Outside in the sun is a great spot if it won't blow away. What happens after all the water has **evaporated**? What is left on your paper?

WHAT'S HAPPENING?

Have you ever gone swimming in the ocean and then licked your lips later in the day? Did they taste salty? The same thing that happened in your experiment happened on your body! The water evaporated and left behind all the salt.

WORDS TO KNOW

mixture: a substance that has two or more different kinds of materials mixed together but not bonded together. Mixtures are easily separated into their parts.

evaporate: when a liquid changes into a gas, causing the original substance to dry out.

PROJECT

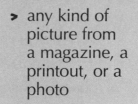

> any kind of picture from a magazine, a printout, or a photo
> glue
> cardboard or cardstock
> scissors

You know that solids hold their shape. But if they're chopped up, have they really changed? Use this activity to find out.

1 Using the glue, attach your picture to the cardboard or cardstock paper.

2 Cut around the entire picture up into piece of different shapes. Shuffle the pieces.

3 You've created a custom puzzle. When you re-assemble it, has the overall picture changed from what it was before? Are solids still the same matter, even after getting broken into little pieces?

WORDS TO KNOW

vibrate: to move back and forth very quickly.

DID YOU KNOW?

Even if you don't see a solid moving, its molecules are! If you took a super-powered microscope and looked at a rock, you'd see the molecules **vibrating** a little. When the rock is cold, the molecules vibrate more slowly. And when the rock gets hot, they move around even more!

PROJECT

- measuring cup
- saucepan
- water
- sugar
- stove
- spoon

When you measure a solid, you can be pretty sure it's going to stay the same size—unless something changes, of course. With this experiment, you can see how the volume of sugar changes, and then use the results as a sweetener! **Caution: An adult needs to help with the boiling water.**

1 Measure 1 cup (236 milliliters) of sugar and pour it into the saucepan.

2 Measure 1 cup (236 milliliters) of water and pour it into the saucepan.

3 Have an adult help you heat the mixture over high heat until boiling, then stir until all of the sugar is completely dissolved. Let the sugar syrup cool.

4 Measure the results. You know that one plus one equals two, right? How much syrup do you have? What might have happened that could have changed the volume of your mixture? Is there anything else in a cup of sugar besides sugar?

TRY THIS! Keep your syrup in a covered container in the fridge, and use it to make lemonade or iced tea. Because the sugar is already dissolved in the syrup, you won't have the grainy texture in your drinks the way you sometimes do when you stir sugar into a cold drink.

PROJECT

Do you like to jump into a swimming pool or a lake in the summer? Doesn't it taste good to sip hot chocolate in the winter? Liquids are all around you! From chilly to steaming hot, you can play in them, drink them, and wash up with them.

You've learned that liquids are one of the forms of matter. They're different from solids and gases because of how closely their molecules are bonded together. In a solid, molecules are tightly packed together, and in a gas the molecules drift pretty far apart. In a liquid, the molecules hover somewhere in between—not as close as in a solid and not as far apart as in a gas.

Suppose someone asks you to draw a picture of a liquid. You might draw a cup of soda, or maybe a picture of a whole lake. Liquids are tricky because they don't really have one shape of their own. They always take the shape of the container they're in.

Imagine a jar full of gumballs compared to a bag with a handful of gumballs. Think of the gumballs as molecules. In the jar, the gumballs aren't going to move around very much. The jar is like a solid. But in the bag, the gumballs can move a lot more, just like molecules in a liquid.

Liquid **flows** around until it bumps into a solid, and then it flows around or inside that solid. That's because liquid takes on the shape of its solid container. It's one of the special properties of liquids.

Liquids have other special properties. Many liquids will freeze when they get cold enough. And some of them will turn into a gas when they get hot enough.

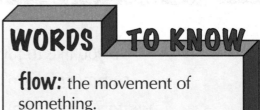

WORDS TO KNOW

flow: the movement of something.

SHAPED ICE

Because water flows to take on the shape of the solid it is in, you can make really cool ice cubes. Get a special ice cube tray in the shape of movie characters or sports equipment or flowers. The water will fill the ice cube tray compartments. When it freezes, you will have shaped ice.

DIFFERENT TYPES OF LIQUIDS

If someone says to you, "Fast! Name a liquid!" what's the first thing you'll think of? Is it water? That's a great answer, because water is the most **abundant** liquid on planet Earth. In fact, more than 70 percent of the Earth's surface is covered in water!

But water is not the only liquid. There are things you typically think of as liquid, such as the things you drink. Milk, soda, juice, and hot chocolate are all liquids. But a liquid doesn't have to be as runny as those.

Honey, syrup, and oil are also considered liquids. While they don't flow as fast as water, they still have the same properties. They take the shape of any container they're in because their molecules are loosely related to each other.

WORDS TO KNOW

abundant: having lots of something.

You think you're a solid, right? It turns out, around 60 percent of the human body is actually LIQUID!

DID YOU KNOW?

Liquids can be thick or thin, hot or chilly, and any color. Some are safe to drink, others are absolutely not. Some mix together easily, others don't. Some liquids help you do things—such as power through dirt—but others simply get you wet!

25

ACIDS AND BASES

Hot and cold are two extremes that describe the temperature of a liquid. **Acids** and **bases** are two extremes that describe how a substance reacts in a liquid by rearranging its atoms. A liquid's acidity is a property of that liquid. All liquids fall somewhere on the range of acids and bases. Right in the middle of these two extremes is distilled water, which is **neutral**.

WORDS TO KNOW

acid: a substance that loses hydrogen in water. Examples include lemon juice and vinegar. Acids can taste bitter, tart, or sour.

base: a substance that loses hydrogen and oxygen in water. Examples include baking soda, soap, and ammonia.

neutral: a liquid that is neither an acid nor a base.

What is the difference between an acid and a base? Acids and bases are groups of substances. Their molecules react in different ways when dissolved in water. When an acid is dissolved in water, the element hydrogen is released. When a base is dissolved in water, hydroxide molecules of hydrogen and oxygen are released.

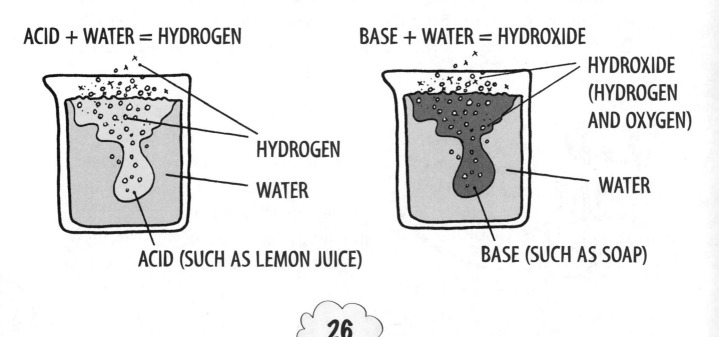

ACID + WATER = HYDROGEN

HYDROGEN

WATER

ACID (SUCH AS LEMON JUICE)

BASE + WATER = HYDROXIDE

HYDROXIDE (HYDROGEN AND OXYGEN)

WATER

BASE (SUCH AS SOAP)

Examples of acids are lemon juice and vinegar. Examples of bases are things such as soap, baking soda, and household ammonia. How can you tell an acid from a base? With a **litmus test** that uses special colored paper. Blue litmus paper turns red when it touches acid. Red litmus paper turns blue when it touches a base.

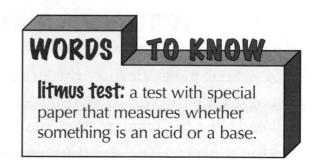

WORDS TO KNOW

litmus test: a test with special paper that measures whether something is an acid or a base.

MIX IT UP!

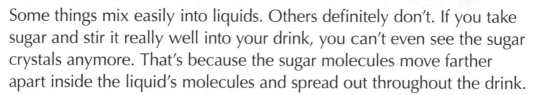

Some things mix easily into liquids. Others definitely don't. If you take sugar and stir it really well into your drink, you can't even see the sugar crystals anymore. That's because the sugar molecules move farther apart inside the liquid's molecules and spread out throughout the drink.

But if you've ever made cake, you may have noticed what happens with two other liquids that don't mix. If you pour water into the bowl with your flour and sugar, then pour oil on top, what happens? The oil kind of rolls off over the water and they stay separate. It's not until you stir them with the other ingredients that they're completely mixed.

But if you took a cup of water and poured oil directly into that, they would never mix. You could shake it up really hard and they'd be foamy and look mixed, but after you let them sit for a while, they'd separate again. Oil will always try to separate out from the water because of the differences in the molecules.

27

ATTRACTING AND REPELLING

A water molecule has three atoms—two hydrogen atoms and one oxygen atom. They're arranged a little like Mickey Mouse's head. One big oxygen atom sits at one end and the two hydrogen atoms are spaced a little apart from each other on the other side of the molecule.

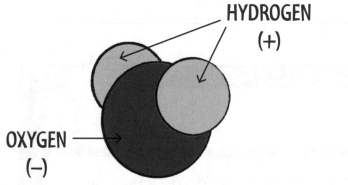

HYDROGEN
(+)

OXYGEN
(−)

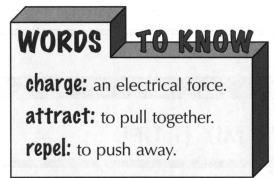

WORDS TO KNOW

charge: an electrical force.

attract: to pull together.

repel: to push away.

The hydrogen atoms each have a slightly positive **charge**. The oxygen atom has a slightly negative charge. That means the entire water molecule itself is positive on one end and negative on the other.

Have you ever played with magnets before? If so, you know that the positive, or plus side, of one magnet will always try to stick to the negative, or minus side, of the other magnet. The positive and negative sides are **attracted** to each other. And the plus side of one magnet will always want to push away the plus side of the other magnet. The positive ends **repel** each other.

That's how charges work. Charges in molecules work the same way as those in the magnets.

Now picture two water molecules, each positive on one side and negative on the other. The positive side of one molecule will be attracted to the negative side of the other water molecule. It's like a magnet.

That is why water molecules want to stick together. They hang on to each other with these very small charges. These are the bonds between water molecules.

Have you ever seen water bugs skating across the surface of water? Why don't they sink? The water molecules at the water's surface are hanging on to each other tightly. The bonds are strong enough that the insect can actually skim right along without breaking those bonds.

But the bonds between the molecules aren't so tight that they can't ever be broken. When water is heated up, those bonds start to break apart. That's when water can evaporate into its gas form.

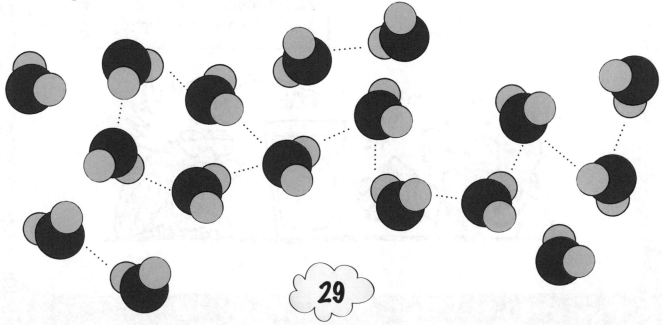

You can measure the impact that different liquid densities have on solids with this project. Start a scientific method worksheet in your science notebook.

1 Fill each container with one of the liquids. You will have several containers, each filled with a different liquid.

2 Form your hypothesis, or prediction. How long do you think it will take your penny or marble to travel through each container of liquid? Create a chart in your science notebook like the one on the next page and fill in an **estimate** for each liquid.

3 Work with a partner to drop a penny or marble into the first liquid at the same second you start the timer.

4 Record on your chart how long it takes for the object to reach the bottom of the container.

> science notebook
> pencil
> 6 narrow, tall containers, such as drinking glasses
> 1 cup (236 milliliters) of each of the following liquids:
  > honey
  > light corn syrup
  > blue dish soap
  > water
  > vegetable oil
  > rubbing alcohol
> 6 pennies or marbles
> timer

WORDS TO KNOW

estimate: to make a close guess.

resistance: a force that slows down another force.

PROJECT

HONEY	LIGHT CORN SYRUP	BLUE DISH SOAP	WATER	VEGETABLE OIL	RUBBING ALCOHOL
ESTIMATE:	ESTIMATE:	ESTIMATE:	ESTIMATE:	ESTIMATE:	ESTIMATE:
ACTUAL:	ACTUAL:	ACTUAL:	ACTUAL:	ACTUAL:	ACTUAL:

5 Repeat steps 1 through 4 with the rest of your liquids.

6 After you've finished, look at your results. Did your object fall at the same speed through all the different layers? Why not? What slowed it down?

WHAT'S HAPPENING? Your solid object weighs the same and has the same mass and density each time. But some liquids are denser than others, because their molecules are more tightly packed together. Denser liquids give objects more **resistance** and slow them down. Can you tell by your results which liquids are denser than others?

TRY THIS! You can explore more by dropping other small objects into your containers, such as raisins, corks, and paper clips. Do some objects sink more slowly? Do some stop sinking partway through the liquid?

If H_2O is water, what is H_2O_4?

LAUGH IT UP!

Drinking, washing, and swimming!

PROJECT

SUPPLIES

> 1 cup (236 milliliters) of each of the following liquids:
  - honey
  - light corn syrup
  - blue dish soap
  - water
  - vegetable oil
  - rubbing alcohol
> several colors of food coloring
> 6 bowls
> slender clear container, such as a vase or graduated cylinder
> spoon or food baster (optional)

Different liquids have different densities. You can show this in a very colorful way with this project.

1 In separate bowls, mix each of the liquids with a different color of food coloring.

2 Once they're all colored, start pouring your liquids into the container in the order listed in "SUPPLIES." The list is from densest to least dense, so be sure you use the right order. This means that the molecules in the honey are more tightly packed than the molecules in the rubbing alcohol.

3 After the honey, you want to carefully pour in each layer without disturbing any layers below. One way to do this is to slowly pour each layer down the side of the container. Another way is to pour the liquid slowly and gently over the back of a spoon held close to the surface. Or, you can use the food baster to suck up each liquid and very gently squirt it down the side of the container for each new level.

4 When you're finished with all the layers, look at your container at eye level. What are the layers doing? Why?

5 Your "artwork" will stay this way as long as you don't shake it up!

> 2 glasses of grape juice
> lemon juice
> baking soda
> spoon

Acids and bases react to each other in different ways. Grape juice is an **indicator**. It will tell whether another liquid is an acid or a base. This indicator will turn blue or red when an acid is present, and green if a base is present. With this project, you can see for yourself what happens when acids and bases mix!

1 Pour a little lemon juice into one glass of grape juice. Stir it up with a spoon. What happens?

2 Now, add two spoonfuls of baking soda to the second glass of grape juice. Stir it in. What happens?

3 Next, stir in some baking soda to your first glass. This is the one you added the lemon juice to. What happens? Why do you think the baking soda had this effect?

WHAT'S HAPPENING? The grape juice turned different colors to indicate whether an acid or a base had been added. When you added baking soda to the grape juice mixed with lemon juice, the liquid turned back to purple. That's because you neutralized the acid with the base—they cancelled each other out.

TRY THIS! Repeat the experiment with fresh grape juice. Add vinegar to one glass and dish soap to the other. Which is an acid and which is a base? Pour out the glasses when you're finished.

WORDS TO KNOW

indicator: a substance that changes color to indicate the presence of another substance.

DID YOU KNOW?

Your body has acids and bases inside! Ammonia is a base found in urine. Your stomach has something called gastric acid that helps break down food.

PROJECT

> science notebook and pencil
> liquid measuring cup
> water
> food coloring
> containers of different sizes and shapes, including a pan such as a baking dish, a drinking glass, a plastic food container, and others
> ruler

Liquids are different from solids in several ways. Liquids take on the shape of the container they're in. Solids don't change shape unless they're cut or changed by some other force. With this activity, you can see how liquids change shape. Start a scientific method worksheet in your science notebook.

1 Pour about 2 cups (473 milliliters) of water into the measuring cup. Add a few drops of food coloring. Pour the water into your first container.

2 Using the ruler, measure how high the water rises in the container. Make other observations, such as how wide across the opening the water spreads, and so on. Note how the water looks in the container. Remember, this is 2 cups of water. Record your observations.

3 Pour the water back into the measuring cup. You shouldn't have lost any water and should still have 2 cups.

4 Now pour the water into your next container, and make the same observations. If you're using the baking dish, for example, the water might only rise up 1 inch (2½ centimeters). But it might be 9 inches (23 centimeters) across the opening. How does this compare to your first container?

5 Continue doing this with the other containers. Each time make sure to start with 2 cups of water. Remember to keep notes! What do you know about liquids that can explain the differences in your measurements?

WHAT'S HAPPENING? You always had the same 2 cups of water. But the water changed shape along with the shape of the container. This could be from very shallow or very deep, or with a lot of surface area as opposed to almost none. That's because a liquid always takes the shape of the container it's in. Even huge areas of water, such as lakes, are shaped by the land that's holding them!

TRY THIS! Turn this into a magic trick. Fill up different-sized containers with the same amount of water. Now challenge a friend to guess which has the most water in it. They may be surprised to find out all the containers have the same exact amount of water!

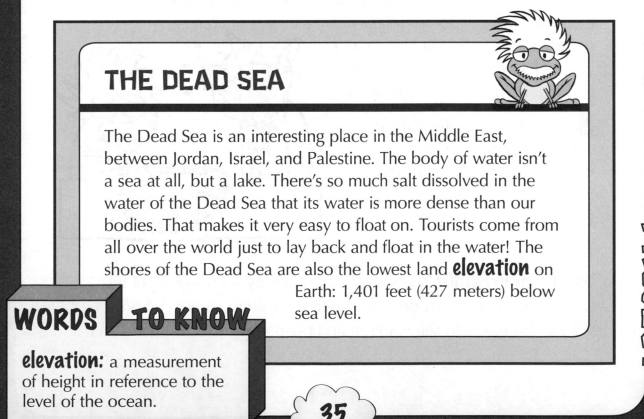

THE DEAD SEA

The Dead Sea is an interesting place in the Middle East, between Jordan, Israel, and Palestine. The body of water isn't a sea at all, but a lake. There's so much salt dissolved in the water of the Dead Sea that its water is more dense than our bodies. That makes it very easy to float on. Tourists come from all over the world just to lay back and float in the water! The shores of the Dead Sea are also the lowest land **elevation** on Earth: 1,401 feet (427 meters) below sea level.

WORDS TO KNOW

elevation: a measurement of height in reference to the level of the ocean.

ON THE SURFACE TRICK

SUPPLIES

> dish soap
> shallow dish filled with water
> salt
> pepper

Although you can easily jump into a swimming pool, the molecules of water actually hold tightly to each other along the water's surface. It's called **surface tension**. You can demonstrate surface tension with this trick that will surprise your friends and family.

1 Secretly coat your pointer finger with dish soap. Have a friend watch while you sprinkle salt and pepper on the surface of the water in the dish. Explain that the grains of salt and pepper don't sink because of the water's surface tension.

WORDS TO KNOW

surface tension: the way the molecules of a liquid hold together tightly at the surface.

2 Tell your audience that you can control the surface of the water and make the salt and pepper move out of your way. Challenge a friend to stick their finger into the water to see if the salt and pepper get out of their way. When your friend puts his or her finger in, the salt and pepper will stick to their finger. Some salt and pepper may sink to the bottom.

3 Now it's your turn. Plunge your finger coated with soap into the water—what happens? What are the soap molecules on your finger doing to the water molecules?

WHAT'S HAPPENING? The soap molecules on your finger repel the water molecules. What does this do to the water's surface tension? Why is this easier to see with salt and pepper sprinkled on the water?

PROJECT

GASES

Suppose you and one hundred other kids are all running around in a huge gym. Now, imagine all the walls of the gym suddenly disappear. What would happen? (Besides everyone being very surprised that the walls just disappeared!) You would probably all spread out even farther.

This is how molecules in a gas behave. They don't cling tightly together the way they do in solids. They don't loosely hang onto each other the way they do in a liquid.

The molecules in a gas freely move around and can easily spread out if there's no container to hold them.

The opposite is true, too. Gas can be forced into a very small container that would never fit the same amount of solid matter or liquid matter. When something is squeezed into a small space by force we call it **compression**.

WORDS TO KNOW

compression: when something is squeezed. Gas can be compressed into a small container by force.

If you've ever seen an adult use "canned air" to clean a computer keyboard, you've seen compression at work. Air is compressed into a small can. When it comes out, it comes rushing out fast because it's under so much pressure. Those molecules want to get out and spread around, and they want to do it fast!

Why didn't the sun go to college?

LAUGH IT UP!

He already had millions of degrees!

There are a lot of ways we use the compression of gas in our lives. A fire extinguisher works because of compression. High air pressure inside the fire extinguisher is what pushes on the foam. It forces the foam to come rushing out to smother flames.

Bicycle tire pumps also use compression of gas to work. First, you pull up on the pump handle to suck air into the chamber. Then, when you push down on the pump, that air is compressed and forced along the hose and into your bike tire.

AIR

IT'S EVERYWHERE!

Gases are present all around you. The biggest example, of course, is air. But air isn't made of just one type of atom. After all, if you look at a periodic table, you won't see air listed. The air in our **atmosphere** is made up of different types of gases.

Are you surprised to learn that air is mostly **nitrogen**? Air also contains oxygen, which is what you need from the air when you breathe. Other gases in the air include small amounts of **argon**, **carbon dioxide**, and others.

WORDS TO KNOW

atmosphere: the mixture of gases surrounding the earth.

nitrogen: an element that is a gas in the air. Nitrogen is the most common gas in air.

argon: an element that is a gas in the air. Argon is used in some light bulbs.

carbon dioxide: an invisible gas that forms when we breathe out. Carbon dioxide is used to make fizzy drinks.

MIX IT UP!

Just as some solids can dissolve into liquids, gases can dissolve into liquids, too. You've most likely seen this in soda. What happens when you twist open the top of a new bottle of soda? You hear that *sssssssssss* noise. If you watch, you can see little bubbles of carbon dioxide gas rise up inside the bottle.

To make soda, or any other fizzy drink, carbon dioxide is forced into the liquid. Then the bottle is closed tightly. Inside the bottle, the gas is under pressure. When you open the bottle, the gas finally has a chance to move around. It starts immediately rising up out of the liquid.

What happens when you leave a bottle of fizzy drink open for a while? When you drink it later on—*blah*! It's flat. All the fizz is gone. This is because all of the gas molecules have worked their way out of the liquid and spread out into the air. All that's left behind is the liquid, with no fizz left at all.

CHANGE ME

Remember how solids and liquids can change their state? A solid can melt into a liquid, and a liquid can freeze or harden into a solid. Gases can change their state too. Gases can change into liquids, and liquids can change into gases.

LAUGHING GAS

You might be given a gas called nitrous oxide before getting a filling at the dentist. Nitrous oxide is a combination of two nitrogen atoms and one oxygen atom that keeps you from feeling pain. It is sometimes called laughing gas because it makes some people laugh. Nitrous oxide is the same gas used to turbo-charge engines in race cars and model rockets.

You see a liquid change into a gas after it rains. When the sun comes out, what happens to those puddles? They disappear because the water evaporates. It turns into water vapor, which is a gas, and spreads out in the air.

WORDS TO KNOW

condense: when water or another liquid cools down and changes from a gas (water vapor) back into a liquid (water).

interact: how things act when they are together.

You can see a gas change into a liquid on a hot summer day. Watch the droplets of water form on the outside of a glass of cold juice on a hot day. That's water vapor in the air **condensing** back into a liquid. You'll learn more about how gases change their form in the next chapter.

UP OR DOWN?

Not all gases are the same. Like liquids, different gases have different densities. That's because different types of molecules **interact** differently. Some stay closer together, making them denser, while others move farther apart, making them less dense.

You know how the bubbles rise up in a fizzy drink? That's because they're lighter than the liquid. They float upward. Can you think of something else that floats upward through the air?

Balloons filled with a gas called helium float up through the air. That's because helium is lighter and less dense than air. If you inflate a balloon with your breath, it just gently floats to the ground when you let it go. But the helium balloons drift upward.

Other gases, such as **propane**, are more dense than air. Propane is used as a fuel in outdoor grills and in stoves and clothes dryers. If you could fill a balloon with propane and drop it from a window, it would drop down through the air.

WORDS TO KNOW

propane: a gas found in natural gas and oil that is burned to produce heat, often in cooking. Propane is heavier than air.

YOW! THAT'S HOT!

The density of a gas can change. Just as the molecules in liquids move farther apart when they're hot and closer together when they're cool, so do gas molecules. If you inflate a playground ball inside, then take it outside on a cold winter day, you'll find that the ball gets a little saggy. That's because the gas molecules inside the ball get closer together in the cold air.

On the other hand, what happens if you inflate a pool raft inside and then go to the beach on a hot summer day? You might find that by the end of the day, it's stretched so tight it seems like it might pop! The heat warms up the air inside the raft, making the molecules move farther apart.

This is what causes the little "done" indicator to pop up on some Thanksgiving turkeys. The heat inside the cooked turkey builds and the pressure pops it up.

BURP!

> warm water
> packet of yeast
> 1 teaspoon (5 milliliters) sugar
> small plastic bottle
> balloon
> science notebook and pencil

There are different kinds of gases all over the universe. You breathe in oxygen and breathe out carbon dioxide. When living creatures expel gas in a fart, it's methane and other gases. With this project, you can see an **organism** called yeast give off gas.

1 Mix some warm water and the dry yeast in a large measuring cup. Stir it around with a fork. Add the sugar and stir that in, too.

2 Pour the yeast-sugar mixture into the bottle. Add more warm water so the bottle is about half full. Swirl the mixture around to mix it up well.

3 Blow up the balloon a couple of times to stretch it, then let the air out. Stretch the neck of the deflated balloon over the opening of the bottle to seal it tightly.

4 Put the bottle someplace warm for about 30 minutes. Start a scientific method worksheet and record your observations. Can you explain what is happening to the balloon? What do you know about liquids and gases that could make this happen?

WORDS TO KNOW

organism: a living thing.

microorganism: an organism so small it can only be seen under a microscope.

WHAT'S HAPPENING? Yeast is a **microorganism** that eats the sugar and releases carbon dioxide. The carbon dioxide gas fills the balloon. Have you ever made bread or pizza dough? When you add yeast to flour and water and feed it with sugar, the dough rises from the carbon dioxide released by the yeast.

PROJECT

43

RAISIN ELEVATORS

Gas bubbles are strong! Watch them flex their muscles as they evaporate from a liquid.

1 Carefully pour the drink into the glass. Try to pour it slowly down the side of the glass. You'll save more of the fizz this way than if you pour it quickly.

2 Gently drop several raisins into the drink. Watch what happens. Do they sink? Do they float? Why are the raisins behaving this way in the liquid?

WHAT'S HAPPENING? Which is more dense, the drink or the raisins? How can you tell? But all those gas bubbles are working hard, and the raisins start rising up through the liquid! The gas bubbles cling to the wrinkles of the raisins. As the gas bubbles float to the surface, they bring the raisin along for a ride.

TRY THIS! Watch and see what happens to the raisins over time. Try dropping other small objects into the drink. What happens?

DID YOU KNOW?

Human farts contain a mixture of gases. Most of the gas is made up of oxygen, nitrogen, carbon dioxide, hydrogen, and methane—but none of those smell! Less than 1 percent of the gas in a fart smells. Scientists think gases such as sulfur are what make a fart smell.

PROJECT

44

> science notebook and pencil
> drinking glass
> water
> flat, stiff coated cardboard or a playing card

A gas doesn't need to be under extreme pressure to be strong. Did you know that all around you at this minute, air is pressing against you? You're so used to the feeling that you don't even notice it. This project will help you see how strong air pressure really is. Start a scientific method worksheet in your science notebook to organize your experiment.

1 Fill the glass with about an inch or two of water.

2 Place the coated cardboard or card on top of the glass. Be sure it completely covers the opening of the glass and extends out over each side. You don't want to be able to see into the glass at all.

3 Hold the cardboard tightly against the glass with one hand. Stand over the sink (or outdoors) and quickly turn the glass upside down. Be sure to keep holding the cardboard tightly over the opening!

4 When the glass is completely upside down (and you're still over the sink or outdoors, just in case!), remove your hand from the cardboard. What happens? Can you explain why?

WHAT'S HAPPENING? Air pressure is what makes this trick work. Because you filled the glass only halfway, the rest of the space in the glass is filled with air. And of course there's air all around you. Air is always pushing down, up, around—everywhere. That's why we have changes in weather, because giant air masses are always moving around the planet. The large amount of air outside the glass pushes harder against the cardboard than the small amount of air inside the glass pushes down on the cardboard.

PROJECT

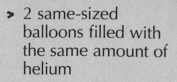

As matter gets colder, the molecules in it move closer together. This happens to matter in any state—solid, liquid, or gas. And when matter gets warmer, the molecules move farther apart. With this activity, you can see how this works in a gas. **Caution: If you plan on doing this experiment outdoors, be sure to hang onto your balloons. Never release balloons into the air. Balloons are harmful to wildlife and pollute the environment.**

> 2 same-sized balloons filled with the same amount of helium
> camera or something to draw with
> 2 long pieces of string
> freezer
> outdoor area or tall stairwell

1 Take a picture of both balloons, side by side, or draw a picture of them. Get a good look at them to make sure they're the same size.

2 Tie a long string to each of the balloons. You want it to be long enough so that when you move to your test area—either outdoors or in a tall stairwell—the balloons will be able to rise pretty far.

What did the boy say after reading a book about helium?

LAUGH IT UP!

"I can't put it down!"

3 Put one balloon in the freezer for at least 20 minutes.

Natural gas is a **fossil fuel** that is burned to produce heat. We use a lot of natural gas in the United States. There are more than 2 million miles of underground pipelines carrying natural gas across the country.

DID YOU KNOW?

WORDS TO KNOW

fossil fuel: a fuel made from the remains of plants and animals that lived millions of years ago. Coal, oil, and natural gas are fossil fuels.

4 When the time is up, remove the balloon from the freezer. Working quickly, document the size of the balloon, either by comparing it to the unfrozen balloon, or taking a picture. Then move quickly to your test area.

5 Hanging on to the strings, release both balloons. Give them room so they don't bump into each other. What happens? Did one rise faster than the other? Why?

WHAT'S HAPPENING? When a gas gets cold, its molecules slow down and move closer together. Why does this make the balloon move differently? Which one is lighter? Is the frozen balloon more dense or less dense?

PROJECT

47

CHANGING STATES OF MATTER

Have you ever put a hot drink in the freezer to cool it down fast? But then maybe a friend came over and you forgot about your drink. By the time you remembered to take your drink out of the freezer, it was frozen solid! The state of matter of your drink changed from a liquid to a solid.

WORDS TO KNOW

chemical reaction: an event that causes the atoms of one or more kinds of matter to rearrange.

The state of all matter can change in many ways. Some of the ways that matter can change might surprise you. Did you know that rocks can melt? Matter can change from solid to liquid, liquid to gas, solid to gas, and back and forth again and again. These **chemical reactions** happen every day. These chemical reactions are going on right around you!

48

SOLID TO LIQUID

In a solid, the molecules are tightly packed together and held by very strong bonds. You've seen that you can break apart some of those bonds using a force such as cutting, pulling, or smashing to change the shape of the solid. But the molecules and the bonds are still the same. That matter is still a solid, even though it's changed its shape.

When a solid changes to a liquid, those molecules no longer share the same strong bonds they had before. They're not packed as tightly together anymore, either.

SOLID	BROKEN SOLID	LIQUID
TIGHTLY PACKED	TIGHTLY PACKED	LOOSELY PACKED

How do those molecules change? Most of the time, it's because of a change in temperature. Different solids have different melting points. When a solid is heated up to its melting point, its molecules are moving fast. The molecules get far enough apart and loosely bonded enough to become a liquid. That's a chemical reaction!

The most common way to see a solid change into a liquid is to watch ice melt. Another common way is to burn a candle. What happens to the candle? As the candle's wax gets hotter, it gets softer and softer until it finally turns to liquid. What do you think is the melting point of ice? Is the melting point of candle wax higher or lower?

WORDS TO KNOW

mineral: a solid, nonliving substance found in nature, such as gold, salt, or copper.

magma: melted rock.

volcano: an opening in the earth's surface through which magma, ash, and gases can burst out.

It's hard to imagine something as hard as rock melting, but it happens! Rock melts under extremely high temperatures and high pressure. But rocks are usually made up of several different **minerals**. Each mineral has a different melting point. So it's a complicated process to melt a rock!

SOLID TO LIQUID

When a rock is melted, it's called **magma**. Magma is the glowing red fluid that erupts from **volcanoes**, so you know it's extremely hot! Deep in the earth, where there's extreme pressure and temperatures, melting rock happens naturally.

Metal is a shiny kind of rock. Jewelers and artists and other people working with metal can melt different metals to pour into molds. This is how metal can be made into different shapes, such as pennies, nickels, and dimes.

LIQUID TO SOLID

A solid that has melted into a liquid can return to a solid state. You know water can freeze into solid ice when the temperature gets cold enough.

When wax that drips down the side of the candle gets far enough from the flame, it starts to cool. And when it gets cool enough, it hardens back into solid wax.

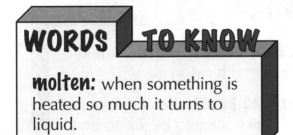

WORDS TO KNOW

molten: when something is heated so much it turns to liquid.

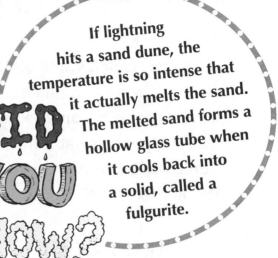

DID YOU KNOW?

If lightning hits a sand dune, the temperature is so intense that it actually melts the sand. The melted sand forms a hollow glass tube when it cools back into a solid, called a fulgurite.

Glass sculptures are curling, delicate, colorful works of art. These are the beautiful results of a liquid that hardened into glass. Drinking glasses are made by melting sand and other ingredients into **molten** glass that hardens as its temperature drops again.

LIQUID TO SOLID

Most of the time, things change from liquid to solid because the temperature drops—think of milk and other ingredients turning into ice cream when they're frozen. But sometimes adding heat can turn something from a liquid to a solid. Think about what happens when you fry an egg. It turns into a solid you can eat!

LIQUID TO GAS

A process called **vaporization** can turn a liquid into a gas. When a liquid is heated so much that it boils, the molecules move around so fast that it becomes a gas. The temperature at which a liquid begins to boil is called its **boiling point**.

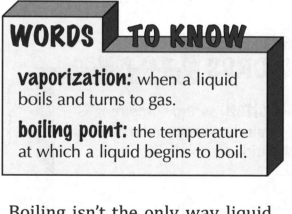

WORDS TO KNOW

vaporization: when a liquid boils and turns to gas.

boiling point: the temperature at which a liquid begins to boil.

LIQUID TO GAS

Boiling isn't the only way liquid can become a gas, though. Water is a great example of this. If you spill water on a flat driveway on a sunny day, the water will quickly evaporate, turning from liquid water to water vapor, a type of gas. The water turns to gas without boiling first.

GAS TO LIQUID

When water vapor or other gases start to cool down, the molecules slow down. If the gases cool down enough, the molecules get close enough together to form bonds. That's when the gas starts condensing, turning back into a liquid.

Natural gas is often cooled to its liquid state to make it easier for companies to move it. The liquid form of the gas takes up much less space, so more of it can fit into a tank. Then the liquid can be changed back into gas to be used in grills, stoves, and to heat buildings.

GAS TO LIQUID

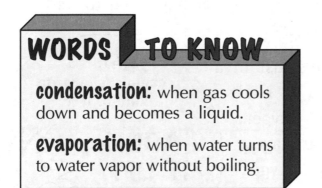

WORDS TO KNOW

condensation: when gas cools down and becomes a liquid.

evaporation: when water turns to water vapor without boiling.

You can see the results of **condensation** and **evaporation** in the weather. When water evaporates into the air, where does it go? It rises, and if there is enough water vapor in the air, it will condense, forming tiny water droplets in clouds. When the clouds meet cooler air, it starts to rain or snow and the water returns to the earth.

SOLID TO GAS

So what about a solid turning to gas? Is that possible? It sure is! It's called **sublimation**.

SOLID TO GAS

What happens when you burn a piece of wood? The wood gets smaller and smaller, until all that remains is ashes and maybe a small, charred bit. Did the wood disappear? What happened to its matter?

That matter is still around—it's just in a different form. It's a gas. Wood is made mostly of carbon, hydrogen, and oxygen. When you light wood on fire, you start a chemical reaction that brings more oxygen into the mix.

What is a chemist's favorite kind of tree?

LAUGH IT UP!

A chemistree!

When you add oxygen molecules to carbon, hydrogen, and oxygen, they become gases. Those gases enter the air as the wood burns. Fire changes the wood's state from a solid to a gas.

CHANGING STATES OF MATTER

GAS TO SOLID

When you look outside on a cold winter morning and see snow blanketing the ground, what's the first thing you think? It's probably not, "Hey! A gas turned into a solid overnight!" But that's what happened.

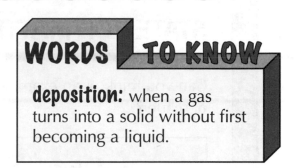

WORDS TO KNOW

deposition: when a gas turns into a solid without first becoming a liquid.

GAS TO SOLID

Up in the clouds, it was cold enough for water vapor (a gas) to freeze directly into snowflakes (a solid). It didn't first become liquid water.

When there's frost on the ground, or frost crystals on your window on a cold day, the same thing happened. When a gas turns to a solid, the process is called **deposition**.

ALL HAIL HAIL!

Have you ever been outside on a warm, rainy day and gotten bonked on the head with hail? Hail starts as tiny clumps of ice formed in thunderclouds. Instead of falling straight to the ground, they get carried up and down by the wind, passing through layers of cool air and warm air. In the warm air, liquid raindrops attach to the ice, and in the cool air, those raindrops freeze solid. Eventually the hailstones are too heavy for the wind and they fall to the ground.

STATES OF MATTER CHART

Can you think of an example of each of these changes in the states of matter?

CHANGE	PROCESS
Solid to liquid	Melting
Liquid to solid	Cooling or Freezing
Liquid to gas	Vaporization (boiling or evaporation)
Gas to liquid	Condensation
Solid to gas	Sublimation
Gas to solid	Deposition

There's no better way to experience a liquid changing to a solid than with homemade ice cream! Do this activity with your friends for extra fun.

1 Mix together the half & half, sugar, and vanilla extract in a bowl. Pour the mixture into the sandwich-size plastic bag. Seal it up tightly and double check the seal. You don't want a leak!

2 Put the ice, salt, and the smaller bag into the larger bag. Seal the larger bag.

3 Start shaking! Keep shaking until the ice cream is firm. This takes about five minutes for soft ice cream.

4 When it's ready, remove the inner bag, stir in the add-ins, and enjoy! What do you know about solids and liquids that explains what happened to your liquid?

- 1 cup (236 milliliters) half & half
- 2 tablespoons (30 milliliters) sugar
- ½ teaspoon (2.5 milliliters) vanilla extract
- bowl and spoon
- sandwich-size Ziploc bag
- ice cubes
- ½ cup (118 milliliters) rock or kosher salt
- gallon-size Ziploc bag
- add-ins such as chocolate chips, rainbow sprinkles, or fruit pieces

THE STATE OF FOOD

There's a trend in the food world called molecular gastronomy. Chefs experiment with chemistry to change the state of food. They can make lemon air, spinach foam, mozzarella balloons, and tiny gel bubbles of olive oil!

PROJECT

- science notebook and pencil
- glass jar
- very hot water
- plate
- ice cubes

Farmers sometimes wish they could make it rain when the weather is too dry and hot. You can't really do that, but with this project you can recreate the conditions that actually do make rain. **Caution: Have an adult help with the hot water.**

1 Start a scientific method worksheet in your science notebook.

2 Fill the jar halfway with hot water. Place the plate on top of the jar.

3 Place the ice cubes on the plate. What do you think will happen? Stand back and watch. Record your observations in your scientific method worksheet. What do you know about liquids and gases that explains what you see?

WHAT'S HAPPENING? Do you notice raindrops gathering? This is similar to what happens in the air to form rain. When warm air and cold air meet, water vapor in the warm air condenses. It changes back into water and falls to the ground as rain.

NOW THAT'S COLD!

Many gases have to be very cold to turn into liquid. Nitrogen turns into liquid at about -346 degrees Fahrenheit (-210 degrees Celsius). That's COLD! Compare that to water, a liquid that freezes into a solid at 32 degrees Fahrenheit (0 degrees Celsius).

PROJECT

T"RUST" ME

> steel wool or a steel scrubbing pad
> shallow bowl
> vinegar
> paper towel
> plate

Matter can change and still remain in the same state. Think about an old nail—it's probably rusty. But it didn't start out that way. Over time, the iron in the nail changes to rust because of a chemical reaction between the iron, the air, and moisture.

Iron and rust are both solids, but they're completely different substances. With this project, you can see iron change to rust.

1 If you're using a steel scrubbing pad, try to rinse and squeeze as much soap out as possible before starting the experiment.

2 Put the steel wool in the bowl and cover it with vinegar. Let it sit for a couple of minutes.

3 Put the paper towel over the plate.

4 Gently squeeze the vinegar out of the steel wool. Then put the steel wool on the paper towel and wait about an hour. Do you notice any changes in the steel wool? What do you see? Why do you think the steel wool changes?

WHAT'S HAPPENING? Within an hour, you'll see a change on the paper towel underneath the steel wool. The steel wool itself will start to change, too.

The vinegar removes the protective coating from the steel wool, and the iron inside begins interacting with the oxygen in the air. Rust is made from iron molecules combining with oxygen molecules. What is happening to your steel wool?

PROJECT

59

Imagine you're sitting around the campfire, roasting marshmallows. If you don't pay attention, your marshmallow will get too gooey and fall off into the fire! What if thunder suddenly rumbles and lightning lights up the sky? You and your family will have to quickly pack up and head for safety until the storm passes.

You know the gooey marshmallow turned from a solid to a liquid. You know the chair you're sitting on is a solid, and the air you're breathing is a gas. But solids, liquids, and gases are not the only states of matter.

What about the fire? Is fire a solid? Is it a liquid? A campfire is a mixture of very hot gases. These gases are a result of a chemical reaction of heat and the elements in the wood.

What about the lightning? That's another story. There are more than just the three states of matter that you have learned about—solid, liquid, and gas. Lightning is in another category called **plasma**.

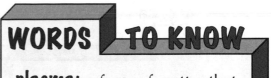

WORDS TO KNOW

plasma: a form of matter that is similar to gas. Plasma can carry electricity.

UH . . . WHAT'S PLASMA?

Have you noticed that hot materials glow? Think about a fire or the filament in a traditional light bulb. Plasma is a form of matter that glows because it is at an extremely high temperature.

Plasma shares some of the same properties as gas. It doesn't have a definite shape unless it's enclosed in a container. But the atoms of plasma are different from gas.

Plasma is made up of positively and negatively charged particles. Because of these charged particles, plasma carries an electrical charge. That's why lightning can start a fire, or affect the electrical circuits in a building if the building gets struck.

DID YOU KNOW?

Liquid is the most common state of matter on the earth because there is so much water. But plasma is the most common state of matter in the universe.

Gas can become plasma from a massive difference in electrical charge between two points. That is what happens in lightning. Another way gas can become plasma is by being exposed to extremely high temperatures, such as those in **nuclear reactions**.

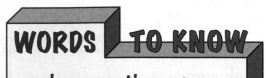

WORDS TO KNOW

nuclear reaction: when atoms fuse together or split apart. This releases a large amount of energy.

Stars and the sun have plasma created by nuclear reactions. But you can create

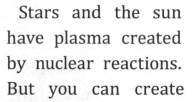

PLASMA

ZAP!

SCUFF SCUFF

your own plasma. Have you ever shuffled across the carpet in dry weather with socks on, then touched a metal doorknob? If you have, you've probably gotten that little zap on your finger from a spark. Guess what? It's plasma!

DID YOU KNOW?

You have something called plasma in your body. But it's not the same as the fourth state of matter called plasma. Blood plasma is a liquid that helps transport blood cells.

NEWTON WHO?

Now you know there are four major forms of matter—but those aren't the only ones! There are other forms of matter that don't exactly follow the properties of solids, liquids, gases, and plasmas.

Can you imagine being able to walk across a liquid? You can, if you're walking on a **non-Newtonian fluid**.

Isaac Newton was an English scientist and mathematician who was born in the 1600s. He made a huge impact on science with his ideas and discoveries.

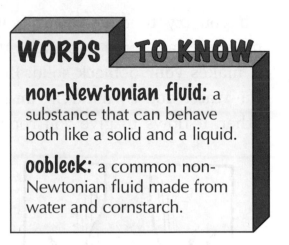

WORDS TO KNOW

non-Newtonian fluid: a substance that can behave both like a solid and a liquid.

oobleck: a common non-Newtonian fluid made from water and cornstarch.

One of the things he studied is how fluids behave. Non-Newtonian fluids act very differently from typical liquids.

With a non-Newtonian fluid, the atoms act differently under different situations. Sometimes the non-Newtonian fluid acts like a liquid. Other times it acts like a solid! This happens without freezing or melting because it happens with no change in temperature.

The most common non-Newtonian fluid is usually called **oobleck**. It is a mixture of cornstarch and water. If you stir just a small spoonful of cornstarch into a large bowl of water, the cornstarch mostly dissolves into the water like many solids. Its molecules spread out into the water. But the more cornstarch you add, the less space there is between its molecules. When the space between the cornstarch is smaller than a piece of cornstarch itself, you've got oobleck, a non-Newtonian fluid.

If you try to punch your bowlful of oobleck, the cornstarch molecules all bump into each other and lock together, like a wall. It makes your oobleck solid. But if you ease your finger into it, the water and cornstarch can move around and slide over each other. It flows to give you room.

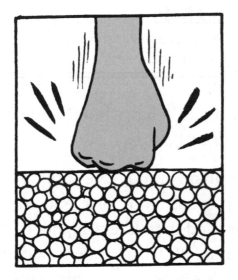 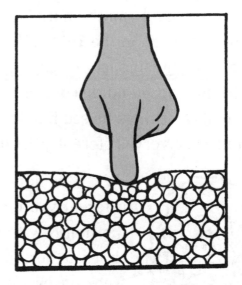

Quicksand is an example of a non-Newtonian fluid. If you're stuck in quicksand and move quickly, you'll get more stuck. But if you move very slowly and carefully spread out your arms and legs, you can pull yourself free.

DID YOU KNOW?

Non-Newtonian fluids act this way because of their structure. The harder the force affecting it, like a punch, kick, or something dropped, the more it acts like a solid. But the gentler the force, the more it acts like a liquid.

THE SAME, BUT DIFFERENT

Not all non-Newtonian fluids react the way oobleck reacts. Ketchup, and yogurt are also examples of non-Newtonian fluids. Have you ever tried to get ketchup out of the bottom of a glass bottle? You shake and shake, and not much happens. Then you turn it upside down and *thunk* it several times on the bottom—the ketchup flows, all right. Once it starts coming out, suddenly you can't stop it! It floods all over your fries! That's because ketchup is in a semi-solid state when it is at rest, but once you start applying a force, it starts flowing. It's the opposite of oobleck, which gets harder when a force is applied to it.

Ketchup and oobleck represent different types of non-Newtonian fluids. Some, such as ketchup, act more like a liquid with a force, while others, get stiffer with a force. What happens when you whip egg whites? Do they get stiffer or more liquidy?

It's easy to make your own oobleck. You just need two ingredients! Explore its properties in as many ways as you can think of. **Caution: When you are finished with your oobleck, either throw it in the garbage or make it very, very runny with a lot of hot water before pouring it in the sink. You don't want to clog the drain with thick oobleck.**

1 Start a scientific method worksheet in your science notebook. Cover your workspace with newspaper. Oobleck can get messy!

2 Put the water in the container. Start adding the cornstarch, a little at a time, stirring slowly and carefully.

3 Keep adding the cornstarch until the oobleck is thick and gooey. At some point, you may want to give up stirring with the spoon and just mix it with your hands. Once the oobleck is ready, it's time to start experimenting!

4 What happens when you put a penny or marble on the surface? Is it different than if you throw it at the oobleck? What if you put something else on top, like a string?

5 Pour the oobleck into a rimmed cookie sheet and set it on a speaker. Then turn the volume up on the speaker and play music. What happens when the music has a lot of bass? What if it's just playing softly?

- science notebook and pencil
- newspaper
- 1 cup (236 milliliters) water
- plastic container
- 1½ to 2 cups (354 to 473 milliliters) cornstarch
- spoon
- items to experiment with, such as pennies, marbles, and string
- rimmed cookie sheet

DID YOU KNOW?

Oobleck got its name from a 1949 Dr. Seuss book called *Bartholomew and the Oobleck.* In the book a little boy battles a mysterious blob!

PROJECT

6 Grab the oobleck with your hand and squeeze a fist. What happens when you clap? If you keep clenching it? If you slowly open your fingers?

7 Try rolling it into a ball. What happens when you stop rolling it?

8 Poke the oobleck hard with your finger. Then try poking it gently. What's the difference in the oobleck? Record your observations in your science notebook! Why does oobleck behave in this way?

TRY THIS! With your parent's permission, mix up a big batch of oobleck and put it in a medium-sized plastic tub. Try to walk on it. Do you need to walk fast or slow to get across? Can you imagine a car driving on the oobleck? Can you think of some new car designs that would help the vehicle cross a pond of oobleck?

DYNAMIC FLUID

You've learned how a solid holds its shape, while other states of matter take on the shapes of their containers. Liquid, gas, plasma, and non-Newtonian fluids are all fluids. A fluid is anything that can flow! Most of the matter in the universe is a fluid. There are even a few planets made of fluids, including Jupiter and Saturn—these are called gas giants. Gravity keeps these planets from flowing apart.

Oobleck isn't the only non-Newtonian fluid in town. Here's a different one to explore—slime! You can substitute white glue for the glue gel if that's all you have, but the glue gel will give you a clear slime. You'll be making two separate **solutions** and then mixing them together.

> 3 plastic containers
> hot water
> measuring cups
> borax such as 20 Mule Team
> 4-ounce (118 milliliters) bottle glue gel
> food coloring (optional)

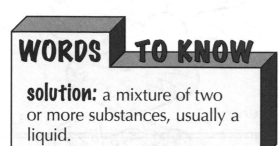

WORDS TO KNOW

solution: a mixture of two or more substances, usually a liquid.

1 For the first solution, put ½ cup (118 milliliters) water into a container and slowly stir in borax. Stop adding the borax when it stops dissolving into the water. You'll know you've reached this point because the borax will start settling at the bottom and won't dissolve. Set this solution aside.

2 For the second solution, put 1 cup (236 milliliters) of water into a separate container. Stir in the glue until it's well mixed. If you want to add food coloring, you can do it now.

Why are chemists so great at problem solving?

LAUGH IT UP!

They have all the solutions.

PROJECT

3 In a third container, mix together ⅓ cup (79 milliliters) of the borax solution and 1 cup (236 milliliters) of the glue solution. Use your hands if it's too hard to mix!

4 Once the slime is mixed together, you can start experimenting with it. Perform the same experiments as you did on the oobleck. How is this non-Newtonian fluid different from the oobleck? How is it the same? Can you think about how the molecules in this slime must be different than the molecules in oobleck for it to behave the way it does?

TURN IT ON!

Here on Earth, there are a lot of human-made plasmas. Fluorescent and neon lights are one place you'll find plasma. Inside the light tube is a gas that carries electricity. When the light is turned on, the gas gets charged up and creates light. An arc welder uses a plasma torch to connect two pieces of metal. The light generated in the process is so bright that the welder has to wear a very dark mask to protect his eyes. Some television screens are plasma, too.

There is not a lot of natural plasma here on Earth, but in space there's plasma everywhere. Scientists think about 99.9 percent of the universe is in a plasma state!

> spoon and small bowl
> ½ teaspoon (2.5 milliliters) sea salt
> 1 teaspoon (5 milliliters) baking soda
> peppermint oil (or any other flavor you like)
> water
> toothbrush

Not all non-Newtonian fluids are just for fun. Some are actually useful! You can make your own non-Newtonian fluid toothpaste with this simple recipe.

1 Using the back of a spoon, finely grind the sea salt into a powder in a small bowl.

2 Add the baking soda and a drop of the oil.

3 Add a couple of drops of water to make a thick paste.

4 Scoop the toothpaste from the bowl onto your toothbrush and use your non-Newtonian fluid to make your pearly whites shine!

ANCIENT TOOTHPASTE

Ancient Egyptians made a type of toothpaste out of **pumice**. These days, most toothpaste is made from an **abrasive** substance to scrub the surface of your teeth, a detergent to clean off stains, and a base to react with the acid left on your teeth from your food. What did you use as an abrasive in your toothpaste? What was your base?

WORDS TO KNOW

pumice: a **porous** rock that is very light.

porous: having lots of tiny holes.

abrasive: a grainy substance.

PROJECT

Have you ever had a lemonade stand? First you make lemonade. You start with a big pitcher of water, squeeze in some lemon juice, add some sugar, and stir. Then you set up your stand, hang up your sign, and wait for the customers to start rolling in.

Congratulations! You started a business, and you also made a mixture! Hardly anyone would stop by if you were selling just water, and even fewer customers would stop if you were selling plain lemon juice. Too sour! But lemon juice, water, and sugar poured over ice? Now that's a mixture that people like—a sweet, refreshing, cooling drink.

Mixtures and COMPOUNDS are combinations of two or more substances. Mixtures and compounds are very similar, and you might not even be able to tell the difference just by looking at them. But they are formed differently. They also behave in different ways.

MIXTURES

You are surrounded by mixtures. The shampoo you use, the pancake batter you cook to make breakfast, even the cat food you pour for your cat. Mixtures are everywhere—and they're not just human-made, either. They occur in nature all the time, such as ocean water, rocks, the soil you walk on, and the air you breathe.

So what is a mixture? A mixture is anything that is a combination of more than one type of element or compound. Those elements or compounds stay the same inside the mixture—they don't change at all. That means they can be removed and exist just as they were before.

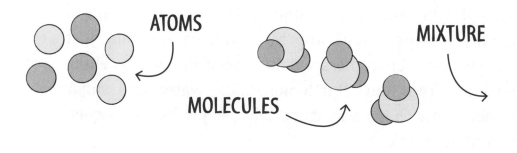

ATOMS

MOLECULES

MIXTURE

Think of it this way: Picture three colors of rope, braided together. When they're braided, they look different than when they're separate. But they're still three separate ropes. All you have to do is unbraid them, and you've separated them.

That's the key thing about mixtures—you can separate them. Suppose you have a small container of sand and you spill a bunch of salt into it. You now have a mixture of sand and salt. But you can separate the sand and salt using **filtration**.

What happens if you pour water into your mixture? The salt will dissolve. When you pour

WORDS TO KNOW

filtration: the process of separating a mixture by sorting out different-sized particles.

the sandy, salty water through a coffee filter, the sand will stay in the coffee filter. The salty water will drip through the coffee filter into a container.

DISSOLVE THE SALT

FILTER THE SAND

You can separate the water and salt, too. If you leave the water and salt mixture sitting on the counter, eventually the water will evaporate. You'll be left with just the salt.

There are many different ways to separate a mixture.

EVAPORATE THE WATER

WORDS TO KNOW

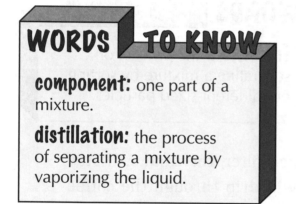

component: one part of a mixture.

distillation: the process of separating a mixture by vaporizing the liquid.

FILTRATION: This is what was used in the sand and salt example. By pouring the mixture through a filter, one **component** (the water) passed through. The water brought the salt with it and left another component (the sand) behind. What if you had different components, such as sand and small shells? You could use a filter with holes large enough to let the sand pass through but not the shells.

EVAPORATION: Waiting for the water to evaporate and leave the salt behind is an example of evaporation. Another, similar method is **distillation**. This is when the liquid is heated up and turned into water vapor or a gas. Distillation leaves behind the solid materials.

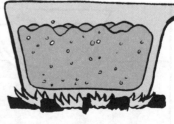

MAGNETS: Suppose you had dumped a bunch of metal marbles in your sand instead of salt? You could have used a big magnet to scan through the sand to pick out the marbles. Have you ever seen those giant cranes in a junkyard? They use a magnet to reach down into the piles of junk to pull out just the scrap metal, leaving the rest behind.

CENTRIFUGE: A **centrifuge** is a machine that spins material around at high speed. The spinning makes denser materials sink to the bottom. The less dense materials rise to the top.

WORDS TO KNOW

centrifuge: a machine that spins mixtures around at high speed. The spinning separates the mixture into its parts.

MAKE IT STRONGER

Another property of mixtures is that you can change the amount of any one of its components at any time. You can always add more sugar to make your lemonade sweeter. Or you can add more lemon juice to make it stronger. The molecules of water, sugar, and lemon juice are all mixing around each other, but they're not creating bonds between each other.

COMPOUNDS

Suppose you have three colors of clay and you squish them all together. Now you have one lump of clay in a weird color. Can you separate them back into their original colors? No. The colors are bonded and will never go back to being three separate colors.

ATOMS

COMPOUND

A compound acts the same as the clay. In a compound, two or more atoms are bonded together to form something different. While a mixture's components can be easily separated, a compound's components are stuck together. The only way a compound can be broken down into its parts is by using a chemical reaction to rearrange the atoms. This doesn't work with all compounds.

When something is a compound, it is identified by how many atoms of each kind of element are present in one molecule of that compound. For example, water is a compound. It's made when two hydrogen atoms bond with one oxygen atom.

Water is written H_2O. The H stands for hydrogen and the O stands for oxygen. The little number 2 next to the H tells you there are two atoms of hydrogen in the compound.

COMPOUNDS VS MIXTURES

What's the difference between a compound and a mixture? A compound is made of two or more elements held together by bonds to form molecules. Compounds are not easily separated. A mixture combines two or more elements or compounds. These elements and compounds stay the same in the mixture and can be separated.

WHAT'S IN A NAME?

All elements are given a special letter or combination of letters to identify them. Some elements are identified by initials from their Latin names. Sodium is *natrium* in Latin, which is why sodium's symbol is Na. Some common elements and their letters are shown here.

ELEMENT	SYMBOL
Oxygen	O
Carbon	C
Hydrogen	H
Sodium	Na
Chlorine	Cl

The gas carbon dioxide has one carbon atom and two oxygen atoms, so it's written CO_2. Table salt is sodium chloride. It's got one atom each of sodium and chlorine, so it's written NaCl.

Table sugar is a compound, too. It's made from carbon, hydrogen, and oxygen. There are 45 atoms in one molecule of table sugar, 12 carbon atoms, 22 hydrogen atoms, and 11 oxygen atoms. Can you write the chemical symbol for table sugar?

Remember how you could stir more lemon juice, water, or sugar into your lemonade and you'd still have a mixture? Compounds aren't like that. You have to follow a very exact recipe to get the right compound.

DID YOU KNOW?

When there is only one atom of an element in a compound, no number is written. So there is no number 1 next to the O in H_2O.

77

IRON CEREAL EXPERIMENT

> measuring cup
> cereal that has been iron fortified, such as Total
> water
> blender
> Ziploc bag
> very strong magnet

Did you know humans eat metal? We can't gobble down spoons or chew on cars, but the human body does need minerals such as iron. Iron is added to some foods, including breakfast cereal. In this project, you can pull the iron out using one of the tools for separating mixtures—a magnet.

1 Put 1 cup (236 milliliters) of cereal and 1 cup of water into the blender. Let it sit, untouched, for about 15 to 20 minutes. You want the cereal to get very soggy.

2 After the cereal is mushy, use short bursts to blend the cereal and water together until you get a soupy mix.

3 Pour the mixture into the plastic bag and seal it tightly.

4 Place the strong magnet flat in the palm of your hand, and place the bag over it. Gently swirl the bag around for a few minutes, keeping your palm as flat as you can. This will help the magnet attract as many of the iron particles as possible.

5 Keeping the magnet held against the bag, carefully flip the bag back over onto your other palm or onto the table. Be sure to keep the magnet against the bag or the iron particles will drift away!

DID YOU KNOW?

All rocks are mixtures of naturally occurring substances called minerals.

PROJECT

6 What happens when you slowly and gently move the magnet around the surface of the bag? Do you see those fuzzy looking black specks? What do you think they are?

WHAT'S HAPPENING? You've just removed the iron from the mixture that was made at the cereal factory.

TRY THIS! Can you separate other mixtures? Try using water to dissolve salt out of sand, for example. How else can you separate mixtures, such as gravel and sand? How about mud, gravel, and water?

TOGETHER WE'RE DIFFERENT

Sometimes, compounds are completely different from the parts that make them up. For example, the element sodium is a metal that is very dangerous. The element chlorine is a gas that's poisonous. But when they combine to form a compound, they make table salt! And table salt is perfectly safe to sprinkle on your French fries.

Think about water again. It's got two atoms of hydrogen and one atom of oxygen. That's all it can ever have and still be water. If you add another oxygen atom, you'll have two hydrogen atoms and two oxygen atoms. You won't have water anymore. You'll have something called hydrogen peroxide. That's what people put on their hair to bleach it white! That's a lot different than putting just water on your hair, and you won't want to drink hydrogen peroxide!

- 4 ounces (118 milliliters) vinegar
- small, empty plastic bottle
- funnel
- balloon
- 2 tablespoons (30 milliliters) baking soda
- toothpick or pencil

A compound is two or more substances that bond together to create a third, new substance. Compounds can't be separated back into their original parts without a chemical reaction. Here's a simple compound you can make yourself.

1 Pour the vinegar into your bottle. Set aside.

BAKING SODA INSIDE

2 Put the end of the funnel into the balloon, and carefully shake the baking soda into the balloon through the funnel. You may need to use a pencil or toothpick to wiggle the baking soda around in the funnel neck if it gets clogged.

3 Make sure the body of the balloon with the baking soda in it is hanging down. Stretch the neck of the balloon over the opening of the bottle.

4 When you're ready, flip the body of the balloon over and hold it up so the baking soda goes down into the bottle and into the vinegar. What happens when the baking soda and vinegar mix? Why would these two substances react in this way?

WHAT'S HAPPENING? In a chemical reaction, the molecules of the baking soda and the molecules of the vinegar rearrange and combine to form a new compound. The solid and the liquid make a gas called carbon dioxide. Carbon dioxide is the compound that makes soda drinks fizzy. What does carbon dioxide do to your balloon?

PROJECT

SALAD DRESSING MIXTURE

You know oil and water don't mix—the oil molecules try to avoid water every chance they get! But they can join together temporarily, with some additional "helper" ingredients. You can see how this works in a delicious way when you make your own salad dressing.

1 Put the dry Italian dressing mix in a medium-sized bowl. Add the rest of the ingredients.

2 Use a whisk to mix everything up. The whisk will help bring your mixture together and spread the oil and water molecules fairly evenly throughout your mixture.

3 Pour the mixture over your favorite salad. If you don't use your mixture right away, store it in a tight container for up to a month. But be sure to give it a good shake or whisk before using, because the oil and water will begin to separate again over time.

- bowl
- packet of dry Italian dressing mix
- ½ teaspoon (2.5 milliliters) dried Italian seasonings
- ½ teaspoon (2.5 milliliters) sugar
- ½ teaspoon (2.5 milliliters) salt
- ¼ teaspoon (1 milliliter) pepper
- ¼ teaspoon (1 milliliter) garlic powder
- 1½ tablespoons (22 milliliters) water
- ¼ cup (59 milliliters) olive oil
- 2 tablespoons (30 milliliters) white vinegar
- ½ teaspoon (2.5 milliliters) mayonnaise
- whisk
- salad

PROJECT

Grab a pencil and a friend to explore all the ideas in this book by doing this silly Mad Lib activity!

noun: a person, place, or thing.
plural noun: more than one person, place, or thing.
adjective: a word that describes a noun.
verb: an action word.
adverb: a word that describes a verb.

As a Matter of Fact

Newt was a mad scientist who lived in _____. One day, his _____ said,

LOCATION ... NOUN

"Quick! I've changed my _____ from a _____ to

NOUN ... ONE STATE OF MATTER

a _____ and I need your help to save it!"

ANOTHER STATE OF MATTER

Newt got in his _____ _____ and _____ to the scene. Sure enough, people

ADJECTIVE NOUN PAST TENSE VERB

were _____ around in shock. "The only way to help is if I use a mixture of _____

–ING VERB ... NOUN

and _____, and _____ it all over him," Newt said.

NOUN VERB

So Newt made the mixture and _____ it all over him. A chemical reaction

PAST TENSE VERB

started instantly! There were _____ _____ shooting everywhere and

ADJECTIVE PLURAL NOUN

people _____ _____.

PAST TENSE ACTION VERB ADVERB ENDING IN –LY

After the smoke cleared, Newt looked. Everything looked okay—except now his

friend was changed from a _____ to a _____ _____!

ONE STATE OF MATTER ADJECTIVE ANOTHER STATE OF MATTER

It's a good thing Newt had studied at _____ and knew all about matter.

SCHOOL NAME

Back to the drawing board!

GLOSSARY

A

abrasive: a grainy substance.

abundant: having lots of something.

acid: a substance that loses hydrogen in water. Examples include lemon juice and vinegar. Acids can taste bitter, tart, or sour.

argon: an element that is a gas in the air. Argon is used in some light bulbs.

atmosphere: the mixture of gases surrounding the earth.

atom: a very small piece of matter. Atoms make up everything in the universe.

attract: to pull together.

B

balance: a device that uses a balance beam to compare masses. It uses an object with a known mass on one side to measure the mass of the object on the other side.

base: a substance that loses hydrogen and oxygen in water. Examples include baking soda, soap, and ammonia.

boiling point: the temperature at which a liquid begins to boil.

bond: the force that holds the atoms in a molecule (or the molecules in a substance) together.

C

carbon dioxide: an invisible gas that forms when we breathe out. Carbon dioxide is used to make fizzy drinks.

centrifuge: a machine that spins mixtures around at high speed. The spinning separates the mixture into its parts.

charge: an electrical force.

chemical reaction: an event that causes the atoms of one or more kinds of matter to rearrange.

component: one part of a mixture.

GLOSSARY

compound: a substance made up of two or more elements. The elements are held together by bonds as molecules. Compounds are not easily separated.

compression: when something is squeezed. Gas can be compressed into a small container by force.

condensation: when gas cools down and becomes a liquid.

condense: when water or another liquid cools down and changes from a gas (water vapor) back into a liquid (water).

D

density: how tightly packed or spread apart molecules are in matter.

deposition: when a gas turns into a solid without first becoming a liquid.

dissolve: when molecules of one substance get mixed into the molecules of another substance.

distillation: the process of separating a mixture by vaporizing the liquid.

E

element: a pure substance that is made of atoms that are all the same.

elevation: a measurement of height in reference to the level of the ocean.

estimate: to make a close guess.

evaporate: when a liquid changes into a gas, causing the original substance to dry out.

evaporation: when water turns to water vapor without boiling.

F

filtration: the process of separating a mixture by sorting out different-sized particles.

flow: the movement of something.

force: a push or a pull.

fossil fuel: a fuel made from the remains of plants and animals that lived millions of years ago. Coal, oil, and natural gas are fossil fuels.

GLOSSARY

freezing point: the temperature at which a liquid changes into a solid.

G

gas: a substance with its molecules freely moving around. A gas will spread out without a container. It can also be compressed into a very small container.

gravity: a force that pulls all objects to the earth.

H

helium: a gas that's lighter than air.

hydrogen: an element that is a gas in the air. It is the most common element.

I

indicator: a substance that changes color to indicate the presence of another substance.

interact: how things act when they are together.

L

liquid: a substance with its molecules loosely packed together. A liquid flows to take the shape of its solid container.

litmus test: a test with special paper that measures whether something is an acid or a base.

M

magma: melted rock.

mass: the measurement of how many atoms are in matter and how tightly packed the atoms are.

matter: anything that takes up space.

melting point: the temperature at which a solid changes into a liquid.

microorganism: an organism so small it can only be seen under a microscope.

GLOSSARY

mineral: a solid, nonliving substance found in nature, such as gold, salt, or copper.

mixture: a substance that has two or more different kinds of materials mixed together but not bonded together. Mixtures are easily separated into their parts.

molecule: a group of atoms.

molten: when something is heated so much it turns to liquid.

N

neutral: a liquid that is neither an acid nor a base.

nitrogen: an element that is a gas in the air. Nitrogen is the most common gas in air.

non-Newtonian fluid: a substance that can behave both like a solid and a liquid.

nuclear reaction: when atoms fuse together or split apart. This releases a large amount of energy.

O

oobleck: a common non-Newtonian fluid made from water and cornstarch.

organism: a living thing.

oxygen: an element that is a gas in the air. People and animals need oxygen to breathe.

P

particle: a tiny piece of matter.

periodic table: the chart that shows all the known elements.

plasma: a form of matter that is similar to gas. Plasma can carry electricity.

porous: having lots of tiny holes.

pressure: a force that pushes on an object.

propane: a gas found in natural gas and oil that is burned to produce heat, often in cooking. Propane is heavier than air.

GLOSSARY

property: a quality or feature of something. The way something is.

pumice: a porous rock that is very light.

R

repel: to push away.

resistance: a force that slows down another force.

S

solid: a substance with its molecules held so tightly together that it holds its shape.

solution: a mixture of two or more substances, usually a liquid.

sublimation: when a solid turns to gas without first becoming a liquid.

substance: a kind of matter.

surface tension: the way the molecules of a liquid hold together tightly at the surface.

T

temperature: how warm or cold something is.

U

universe: everything that exists, everywhere.

V

vaporization: when a liquid boils and turns to gas.

vibrate: to move back and forth very quickly.

volcano: an opening in the earth's surface through which magma, ash, and gases can burst out.

volume: the amount of space a solid takes up.

W

weight: the measurement of gravity pulling down on matter.

RESOURCES

BOOKS

Brandolini, Anita. *Fizz, Bubble & Flash! Element Explorations & Atom Adventures for Hands-On Science Fun!* Williamson Publishing, 2003

Brown, Jordan. *Crazy Concoctions: A Mad Scientist's Guide to Messy Mixtures.* Imagine, 2012

Dingle, Adrian. *The Periodic Table: Elements with Style!* Kingfisher, 2007

Garrett, Ginger. *Solids, Liquids, And Gases (Rookie Read-About Science).* Children's Press, 2005

Green, Dan. *Basher Science: Chemistry: Getting a Big Reaction.* Kingfisher, 2010

Leavitt, Loralee. *Candy Experiments.* Andrews McMeel Publishing, 2013

Newmark, Ann. *DK Eyewitness Books: Chemistry.* DK Children, 2005

Spangler, Steve. *Naked Eggs and Flying Potatoes: Unforgettable Experiments That Make Science Fun.* Greenleaf Book Group Press, 2010

VanCleave, Janice. *Janice VanCleave's Chemistry for Every Kid: 101 Easy Experiments that Really Work.* Jossey-Bass, 1989 (older but still excellent)

RESOURCES

WEBSITES

Chem4Kids is an introduction to chemistry for kids with plenty of ways to get in-depth and explore more: **www.chem4kids.com**

Adventures in Chemistry is hosted by the American Chemical Society and has plenty of information and experiments for kids to explore: **www.acs.org/content/acs/en/education/whatischemistry/adventures-in-chemistry.html**

An interactive periodic table of elements: **www.chemicalelements.com**

Science of Cooking will let kids explore how chemical interactions make great food: **www.exploratorium.edu/cooking/index.html**

In-depth look at pH: **www.miamisci.org/ph**

Ducksters science site, exploring chemistry for kids: **www.ducksters.com/science/chemistry**

Chemistry for Kids explores solids and liquids in depth, along with bonds, atoms, and more: **www.chemistryforkids.net**

Explore chemical formulas and find out how many molecules are in different compounds with this interactive site: **www.zerobio.com/drag_gr9/chem.htm**

A song about the elements: **www.allperiodictables.com/aptpages/apt_1_CC_Lehrer.html**

INDEX

INDEX